CENGAGE Learning

Nonfiction Classics for Students, Volume 1

Staff

Editor: Elizabeth Thomason.

Contributing Editors: Reginald Carlton, Anne Marie Hacht, Michael L. LaBlanc, Ira Mark Milne, Jennifer Smith.

Managing Editor, Literature Content: Dwayne D. Hayes.

Managing Editor, Literature Product: David Galens.

Publisher, Literature Product: Mark Scott.

Content Capture: Joyce Nakamura, *Managing Editor*. Sara Constantakis, *Editor*.

Research: Victoria B. Cariappa, *Research Manager*. Cheryl Warnock, *Research Specialist*. Tamara Nott, Tracie A. Richardson, *Research Associates*. Nicodemus Ford, Sarah Genik, Timothy Lehnerer, Ron Morelli, *Research Assistants*.

Permissions: Maria Franklin, *Permissions Manager.* Shalice Shah-Caldwell, *Permissions Associate.* Jacqueline Jones, *Permissions Assistant.*

Manufacturing: Mary Beth Trimper, *Manager, Composition and Electronic Prepress.* Evi Seoud, *Assistant Manager, Composition Purchasing and Electronic Prepress.* Stacy Melson, *Buyer.*

Imaging and Multimedia Content Team: Barbara Yarrow, *Manager.* Randy Bassett, *Imaging Supervisor.* Robert Duncan, Dan Newell, *Imaging Specialists.* Pamela A. Reed, *Imaging Coordinator.* Leitha Etheridge-Sims, Mary Grimes, David G. Oblender, *Image Catalogers.* Robyn V. Young, *Project Manager.* Dean Dauphinais, *Senior Image Editor.* Kelly A. Quin, *Image Editor.*

Product Design Team: Kenn Zorn, *Product Design Manager.* Pamela A. E. Galbreath, *Senior Art Director.* Michael Logusz, *Graphic Artist.*

agency, institution, publication, service, or individual does not imply endorsement of the editors or publisher. Errors brought to the attention of the publisher and verified to the satisfaction of the publisher will be corrected in future editions.

This publication is a creative work fully protected by all applicable copyright laws, as well as by misappropriation, trade secret, unfair competition, and other applicable laws. The authors and editors of this work have added value to the underlying factual material herein through one or more of the following: unique and original selection, coordination, expression, arrangement, and classification of the information. All rights to this publication will be vigorously defended.

Silent Spring

Rachel Carson

1962

Introduction

First published in the United States in 1962, *Silent Spring* surveys mounting evidence that widespread pesticide use endangers both wildlife and humans. Along the way, Rachel Carson criticizes an irresponsible chemical industry, which continues to claim that pesticides are safe, and imprudent public officials, who accept without question this disinformation. As an alternative to the "scorched earth" logic underlying accepted pest-control practices, the author outlines the "biotic" approach —cheaper, safer, longer acting, natural solutions to pest problems (for example, controlling the

Japanese beetle by introducing a fungus that causes a fatal disease in this insect).

The primary inspiration for the book was a friend of Carson's who was concerned about dying birds in her hometown where the authorities had sprayed DDT to control mosquitoes. At about the same time, a disastrous pesticide campaign against the fire ant of the Southeast was receiving national attention. Formerly a science writer for the United States Fish and Wildlife Service, Carson already had some acquaintance with research on pesticides, and she was ready to speak out. Originally planned as an article, *Silent Spring* became a book of more than two hundred pages when the only outlet she could find was the book publisher Houghton Mifflin.

Though *Silent Spring* is without question her best-known book today, Carson was already a national literary celebrity when it came out. As work of social criticism, *Silent Spring* represented a considerable departure from the natural history with which she had made a name for herself. Whether this would have been a turning point in her career or merely a detour is impossible to know because Carson succumbed to breast cancer only a year and a half after *Silent Spring* appeared. What is clear, however, is that her public image was irrevocably transformed. Average Americans came to see her as a noble crusader while the chemical industry would quickly spend more than a quarter of a million dollars to discredit her.

Few books have had as much impact on late

twentieth-century life as Carson's *Silent Spring*. Though an environmental consciousness can be discerned in American culture as far back as the nineteenth century, environmentalism as it is known today has only been around for about forty years, and Carson's book is one of its primary sources. Her tirade against humankind's attempt to use technology to dominate nature wrenched environmentalism from its relatively narrow, conservationist groove and helped transform it into a sweeping social movement that has since impacted almost every area of everyday life.

Author Biography

Rachel Louise Carson was born on May 27, 1907, in Springdale, Pennsylvania, the daughter of Robert Warden Carson and Maria Frazier McLean. The family had very little money—Robert Carson made only a slim living as a salesman and utility employee—but thanks to their talented and well-educated mother, Rachel and her older brother and sister enjoyed a comparatively stimulating childhood. A great reader and passionate naturalist, Maria Carson left an especially deep imprint on her youngest child. While still quite young, Rachel began writing stories about animals, and by age ten, she had published a prize-winning magazine piece.

In 1925, Carson earned a scholarship for Pennsylvania Women's College where she hoped to prepare herself for a literary career by majoring in English. As had always been her habit in school, the bright but reserved student focused on academics rather than socializing and was soon one of the college's top scholars. Less expected was Carson's changing her major to biology after taking a class taught by a captivating young zoology professor named Mary Scott Skinner. In 1929, after graduating with high honors, the writer who would someday earn fame for her work on marine life got her first look at the sea as a summer intern at Woods Hole Laboratory on Cape Cod. Later that year, Carson began graduate work in zoology at Johns Hopkins University, but in 1935, when her father suddenly died, family responsibilities put an end to her formal studies. By 1937, she was the sole provider for both her mother and the children of her now deceased sister.

It was at this point that she embarked on her long career as a civil servant, an endeavor that would occupy her for the next decade and a half and the crucible out of which would come the influential nature writing of her later life. Producing publications for the Bureau of Fisheries and the United States Fish and Wildlife Service, Carson increased her already considerable expertise in biology and honed her skills as a writer. The bureaucratic elements of such work do not seem to have been at all stifling; in *Notable American Women,* Paul Brooks credits Carson for setting "a new standard for government publication." It was inevitable that such work would someday come to the notice of a wider circle of readers, as it did in 1941, when she published *Under the Sea Wind,* a work of natural history that originated in an article she had written for a Bureau of Fisheries publication in the late 1930s. Though it was well received by reviewers, the book was something of a false start: the entrance of the United States into World War II led to poor sales, and Carson herself soon had to put other such projects aside to deal with growing responsibilities at Fish and Wildlife. (By 1949, she was editor of all agency publications.)

It wasn't until 1951 that her next and most popular book, *The Sea Around Us*, appeared. It was among the first examples of what was to become an important late twentieth-century genre, science as literature. On the *New York Times* bestseller list for eighty-six weeks, this volume earned Carson enough royalties to enable her to retire from government work and focus on the projects that most interested her.

After completing the third and final volume of her "biography of the sea," *The Edge of the Sea*, and a handful of smaller projects, Carson was prompted by a series of events to write the book that would make her one of the most important women of the twentieth century. Carson was recruited to help a friend from Duxbury, Massachusetts, challenge a state mosquito control program that seemed to be wiping out birds. This and another widely publicized controversy over a similar development in the Southeast led Carson to write on the mounting scientific evidence about the risks of pesticides. Doubting that she could find a magazine that would publish an article on so gloomy a topic, Carson produced an entire book for an interested editor at Houghton Mifflin. Serialized by the *New Yorker* in advance of its 1962 publication, *Silent Spring* became the focus of intense attention, not least because the chemical industry responded with a quarter-million-dollar campaign to discredit the author. Before the controversy cooled, a presidential commission began looking into the problem, and Congress began considering tougher restrictions on dangerous chemicals. (Carson herself testified before Congress.) Already a prize-winning writer, Carson was now elevated to the ranks of the nation's most important public figures. The true magnitude of her accomplishment would only become clear some months later, when Carson died on April 14, 1964, in Silver Springs, Maryland. During the four years that she worked on *Silent Spring*, Carson also had been battling cancer.

Chapter One

Carson's survey of the research on pesticides opens in a most unscientific fashion with a tale about an American town that has suffered a series of plagues. At chapter's end, Carson acknowledges that the town is an imaginary one, but lest the tale be dismissed as mere fantasy, she hastens to add that each of the catastrophes it catalogs "has actually happened somewhere, and many real communities have already suffered a substantial number of them."

Chapters Two and Three

Not until chapter two does Carson identify the source of the ills described in chapter one: potent synthetic poisons of relatively recent design, proliferating at the rate of about five hundred a year, applied in massive quantities virtually everywhere, with disastrous short-and long-term consequences for both wildlife and humans. To convey the grave danger that these substances represent, she introduces an analogy that will resurface over and over in *Silent Spring*: pesticides are like atomic radiation—invisible, with deadly effects that often manifest themselves only after a long delay. Chapter three identifies a small handful of qualities that make the new pesticides so much more dangerous than their predecessors: 1) greater potency 2) slower decomposition and 3) a tendency to concentrate in fatty tissue. Carson clarifies the significance of the last two characteristics by pointing out that a toxin that might not constitute a danger in small doses will ultimately do so if it accumulates in the body, and also that substances with this propensity concentrate as one moves up the food chain.

Chapters Four, Five, and Six

Chapters four, five and six form a triptych that stresses the highly interconnectedness of life in three biological systems—plant systems and those centered in water or soil. Given its fluidity and interconnectedness, water is an extremely difficult place to contain a problem, Carson points out. As an unintended result of runoff from agricultural spraying and of poisons sometimes directly introduced in the water supply, groundwater nearly everywhere is tainted with one or more potent toxins. The full extent of the problem, she worries, cannot even be precisely measured because methods for screening the new chemicals have yet to be routinized. In some instances, the danger lies in substances formed by unexpected reactions that take place between individual contaminants; in such cases, toxins might escape detection even where tests are available. Chapter five explains the life cycle within soil-based ecosystems: rich soil gives rise to hearty plant life; then the natural process of death and decay breaks down the plants, and the soil's vitality is restored. Pesticides threaten this fundamental dynamic—fundamental not just for plants but also for the higher organisms that live on plants. An insecticide applied to control a particular crop—damaging insect depletes the microbial life within the soil that facilitates the essential enrichment cycle, hence the millions of pounds of chemical fertilizer required each year by factory—farms. In chapter six, Carson's focus shifts from insecticides to herbicides. The general picture that emerges is of a deceptive chemical industry and ill—informed public authorities spending large sums of taxpayers' money undermining whole ecosystems to eradicate one or two nuisance species.

Chapter Seven

In "Needless Havoc," Carson's attention turns to the people behind pesticides, the public officials who are responsible for the widespread use of these dangerous chemicals. What has typified their behavior in her view is almost unbelievable recklessness followed by an irrational unwillingness to reckon with the catastrophes they have wrought. Exhibit A is the infamous campaign against the Japanese beetle, a frenzy that swept the Midwest in the late fifties. In the first place, Carson argues, there was no real evidence that the beetle constituted a serious threat. Secondly, officials failed to warn the public of potential risks involved in combating the insect with pesticides.

Chapter Eight

Not surprisingly, at the very heart of *Silent Spring* lies a chapter called "And No Birds Sing," where the author recounts the true stories from whence the book's most unforgettable image comes. The chemical villain in these tragedies is the notorious DDT; the principal victims are the robin, beloved herald of spring, and the eagle, revered symbol of national spirit. That the shrewd writer chose species with so much emotional resonance is hardly an accident. Both birds' fates bring the discussion back to the problem of bio—magnification, the concentration of toxins as they pass from one organism to the next along the food chain: the robin receive fatal doses from consuming poisoned worms and other insects, the eagle from pesticide—carrying fish.

Chapter Nine

Chapter nine explains how blanket pesticide spraying—of forests, crop fields, and suburban lawns—is wreaking havoc on aquatic life in the streams, estuaries, and coastal waters that receive runoff from treated areas. The chapter's most frightening observation is that runoff concentrates in marshes and estuaries where freshwater meets the seas, extraordinarily fragile ecosystems and the primary feeding and spawning grounds for many species—the foundation of much aquatic life.

Chapter Ten

Reviewing two more disastrous eradication efforts, chapter ten sounds many of the same notes as chapter eight. What chapter ten adds to this now fairly well-developed picture is a clearer sense of the colossal blunder that was aerial spraying. Carson reports that pilots were paid according to how much pesticide they sprayed, and so they drenched the countryside with toxic chemicals, contaminating orchards and gardens, killing birds, bees and other wildlife, poisoning milk cows and even soaking humans who happened to get in the way.

Chapter Eleven

Chapter eleven concerns the minute but repeated exposures to pesticides that every man, woman, and child suffers in all but the most isolated regions of the planet. Carson lays the blame for the breathtaking diffusion of dangerous chemicals in everyday life on the deceptive marketing campaigns of pesticide makers, which insist these products are safe, and government agencies like the Department of Agriculture and the FDA, which not only countenance such disinformation but actively promoted the use of synthetic poisons.

Chapters Twelve, Thirteen, and Fourteen

Chapters twelve, thirteen and fourteen focus on

the effects of pesticides on people. Chapter twelve stresses two key issues: first, that pesticides are absorbed by fat, a widely dispersed tissue, and so they insinuate themselves in virtually every part of the system, including the ever so crucial organs and fundamental cell structures; and second, because most people accumulate these toxins by way of repeated minute exposure of which they are rarely aware, it difficult to trace the resulting pathologies to their true cause. Chapter thirteen explains one of the book's main refrains—that pesticides are so very dangerous because they disrupt basic biological processes like oxidation (cell metabolism) and mitosis (cell reproduction). The central claim here is that pesticides are probably responsible for cancer, birth defects, and a wide array of chromosomal abnormalities. Scientific research in this area was still in an early stage when Carson wrote *Silent Spring*, but plant and animal studies were already suggesting what had long been known about radiation, namely that pesticides had powerful mutagenic properties. Chapter fourteen chronicles the history of the carcinogen, a term that has become only more familiar since 1962. It was first surmised that cancer related to environmental conditions in the eighteenth century, when a London physician noted an extremely high incidence of scrotal tumors among the city's chimney sweeps, who were all day covered in soot. During the nineteenth century, with the rise of industry, several other suspicious relationships had been observed. But with World War II and the rise of widespread pesticide use, the risk of cancer confronted not just members of certain occupational groups but virtually everyone.

Chapters Fifteen and Sixteen

Chapters fifteen and sixteen discuss in a comprehensive way one of Carson's most damning criticism of pesticides, but one she has thus far only voiced in passing: not only are pesticides expensive and extremely dangerous, but they are also terribly ineffective. The trouble is twofold. Chapter fifteen focuses on the first part of the problem; current pesticide practice, Carson argues, is like trying to repair a delicate watch with a sledgehammer. Massive applications of highly toxic substances reverberate through whole ecosystems, upsetting delicate balances and often compounding the original problem. Chapter sixteen highlights the tendency of pesticides to lose effectiveness quickly as insects and other nuisance organisms develop resistance. The problem arises from the indefatigable reality of natural selection. Within any given pest species, some number of organisms will be less susceptible to pesticides as a function of ordinary genetic variety within the species. Pesticide kills off the weak, leaving the pesticide— resilient to thrive and establish a new generation of super bugs. Of particular concern is the loss of effective tools in the fight against disease carrying insects like the mosquito.

Chapter Seventeen

Since so many of the book's chapters conclude with some mention of safer alternatives to current pesticide practices, it is hardly surprising that the book itself concludes with an extended discussion of what Carson calls "biotic controls." One of the main arguments of the chemical industry in the face of mounting evidence about the dangers of pesticides is that the risks are justified by benefits to agriculture and other areas. By laying out in fine detail cheaper, safer, and more effective alternatives, Carson pulls the rug out from under the industry with its self—interested talk of pesticide benefits. Broken into three sections, each of which focuses on a slightly different basic strategy, chapter seventeen offers a cogent overview of the elegant science of natural pest control. Part one explains how chemicals derived from the insects themselves can be used as repellants or lures for traps that pose no risk to humans. Part two shows how repeatedly introducing sterilized males into target populations can bring about a gradual decline of pests. And part three reports on the use of natural enemies—bacterial insecticides and predator species—to combat pests.

The Chemical Industry

Because Carson refrains from naming particular corporations, the pesticide makers assume the monolithic shape of an evil empire in *Silent Spring*. Yet Carson does not preach at the industry. Yes, it develops hundreds of new deadly toxins a year, and, through disinformation and pressure on government agencies, it promotes their widest possible use—the book is very clear about these things. But Carson seems to view such activity as natural to the commercial enterprise and wastes no time calling on pesticide producers to reform themselves.

The Government

The government is the other great villain in Carson's story, and though one might think it is the chemical industry that bears primary responsibility for what has occurred, she is much more critical of public servants. Her thinking seems to be that more is to be expected of government. In succumbing to political pressure and helping pesticide makers promote their products, she argues, government has lost sight of its *raison d'etre* (reason for being), protecting the public interest. Carson holds that instead of echoing industry disinformation and spending taxpayers' money on reckless pest eradication programs, agencies like the Department of Agriculture and the Food and Drug Administration ought to impose stricter controls on the development, sale, and use of dangerous chemicals and to fund more research.

Nature

An overview of key figures in *Silent Spring* that did not mention nature would be quite incomplete. In terms of the amount of attention that is devoted to them, plant and animals are the most important "characters" in the book, surpassing humans by a wide margin, who are the focus of just a few chapters. Still, despite the almost infinite variety of life forms that Carson mentions, there emerges a single image of nature that has a crucial function in Carson's case against pesticides: nature as a fabric of life in which all things are connected, from the smallest of soil microbes to human beings and other large mammals. If readers accept such a view, they must also agree with Carson that the sledgehammer-like approach of current pest control —introducing large amounts of extremely toxic chemicals into the environment to eradicate a few species of insects—is indefensible. What poisons one part of the fabric of life poisons the whole.

The Public

Along with wildlife, the public is a major concern in *Silent Spring*. The image the book projects of this collective entity is that of a victim of the chemical industry, betrayed by irresponsible public officials and exposed to toxic pesticides at every turn. As the terrible side effects of pesticides become clearer, the public begins to ask questions, demand answers, and insist on greater responsiveness from government agencies.

The Visionaries

The heroes of *Silent Spring* come from several walks of life: scientists laboring patiently in an often tedious and seriously underfunded area of research to determine the precise scope of the pesticide threat; birders and other amateur naturalists, whose careful observation of wildlife in the field yields essential information about the problem; activists driven by a deep concern for their communities and the natural environment to challenge industry and government to behave more responsibly; and philosophers, writers, and other thinkers who help citizens understand the cultural sources not just of the pesticide problem but of the whole range of trouble that modern civilization has stirred up with technology. What all of these individuals share is an uncommon power discernment. Simply recognizing the broad impact of pesticides on the environment and health is a significant achievement. What makes Carson's visionaries even more remarkable is their having probed this tricky problem with great precision in the face of widespread disinformation and obstruction.

Media Adaptations

- The documentary *The "Silent Spring" of Rachel Carson,* produced by CBS Reports in 1963, captures the mood of the times when the book first appeared.

- In 1993, PBS produced and presented *Rachel Carson's "Silent Spring"* as part of its "American Experience" series. The film features interviews with several of the writer's colleagues and critics.

- Durkin Hayes published an abridged version of *Silent Spring* on audiocassette in 1993. The text is read by actress Ellen Burstyn.

The Science of Pesticides

One of the great insights of *Silent Spring* is its grasp of the pesticide problem as a compound one. On one hand, there are the intrinsic dangers of these chemicals: their capacity to disrupt basic biological processes, their persistence in the environment, and so forth. But Carson knew that the manner in which a dangerous substance is also crucial. To understand how compounds like DDT and malathion have come to threaten life on a global scale, one has to examine what has been done with them. Each of the major themes of *Silent Spring* belongs then to one of two lines of argument; the first concerns the raw toxicity of pesticides, the second the recklessness with which they have been employed.

Along with atomic fallout, the synthetic pesticides that came into wide use after World War II are the most dangerous substances man has ever created. The heart of the problem, science has shown, is the pesticides' unique capacity for disrupting critical biological processes like metabolism and cell division. Acute exposure can cause catastrophic systemic problems—paralysis, immune deficiency, sterility, etc.—and small doses repeated over time can lead to grave illnesses like cancer.

Carson attributes this radically disruptive

potential to the distinctive molecular structure of synthetic pesticides. Part carbon, they mimic the substances that are crucial to life (enzymes, hormones, etc.) and so gain entrance to sensitive physiological systems. Once inside these vital systems, the elements to which the carbon is bound (chlorine and other deadly materials) wreak havoc on the organism.

Two other properties that increase the hazard of pesticides are, first, the slow rate at which they break down and become less toxic, and, second, their tendency to accumulate in fat tissue. It is these characteristics that make even low-level exposure to pesticides so dangerous. A dose that is too small to cause immediate harm is stored in the body and remains active for a considerable period; with each subsequent exposure the cumulative "body burden" increases, and along with it the chance of serious illness. These properties also put species at the top of the food chain at special risk because they absorb large amounts of pesticide from the lower organisms they consume, a process called "biomagnification."

The Culture of Pesticides

Carson takes great pains to show that it is the imprudent use of pesticides, as much as their intrinsic properties, which makes them one of the worst health threats of the twentieth century. Dosing blankets with DDT, spraying densely populated neighborhoods from the air, and pouring pesticide into ponds to kill mosquitoes might have poisoned the planet if not for *Silent Spring*. From the vantage point of a more environmentally conscious age, it is difficult to understand how such practices could have been so popular. Years ahead of her time, Carson was dumbfounded.

Topics for Further Study

- Look carefully at the material on pesticides at the web site of the Environmental Protection Agency (http://www.epa.gov/ebtpages/pesticides Does the government's attitude toward these products seem different today than it was in 1962, as described in *Silent Spring* ? Report your findings in a one-page summary.

- Imagine that it is 1962. Write a one- or two-page letter using what you learned from the book to persuade your state representative or senator to do something about the problem Carson describes. Be sure to tell your representative specifically what you would like him or her to do.

- Identify three passages in *Silent Spring* that seem particularly compelling. Does Carson's language (word choice, tone, images, etc.) contribute something to the force of these excerpts. How? Summarize your observations in a brief essay.

- Examine the labels of some pesticide products around the house, taking note of their active ingredients. At http://www.epa.gov/pesticides/info.htm, see what you can find out about the health hazards of these products. Report your findings in a one-page summary.

As nearly as Carson could figure, mid-twentieth-century attitudes toward synthetic pesticides were warped by a trio of interacting forces: the chemical industry, government, and what she calls "Neanderthal science." In calling science "Neanderthal," she has two characteristics of contemporary methodology in mind. The first is the extraordinarily high degree of specialization.

Knowledge might appear to advance at a faster pace along the narrow paths of modern research, but it has also become more fragmented; the entomologist developing a pesticide to control the hungry gypsy moth, for example, is unlikely to know much about the chemical's harmful effects on non-targeted organisms such as birds and fish. The second defect of science, especially in the applied areas, is its habit of conceiving problems in military terms, an outlook it shared to some degree with culture as a whole in the aftermath of World War II. Solutions are always seen to depend on exerting the greatest possible force over an "enemy." This logic expresses itself in pest management strategies that advocate applying the most lethal substances available in saturating quantities to eradicate entire species. As an alternative to the "total war" approach to solving problems, Carson proposes an approach that exploits the natural tendency of systems to seek balance; with a little help, it has been proven time and time again, the natural environment can solve its own problems cheaply, safely, and effectively. *Silent Spring* recounts some elegant, low-intensity, "biotic" interventions, such as cultivating certain plants to encourage species that compete with pests or introducing a pest-specific disease into a blighted area.

The second major culprit behind the overuse of pesticides is the chemical industry itself. The corporate giants use their enormous political leverage to co-opt government agencies and engage in large scale disinformation campaigns to defuse growing public concern about synthetic poisons. To a certain degree, the short-sightedness of science described above is itself a product of industry influence: because pesticide makers are the largest funders of research in the field, most investigation tends to harmonize with corporate interests; hence the paucity of knowledge about the risks of synthetic chemicals and the limited effort to develop safer, "biotic" alternatives. It is worth noting that, as outrageous as the posture of the industry might appear to some, Carson eschews moralistic argument to make a case that is all the more compelling for its sheer pragmatism. Pesticide makers, she concedes, will always have as their sole concern the profitable sale of pesticides. But if it is absurd to expect them to take a broader view, she concludes, it is just as unreasonable to allow them any role in the process by which public policy on pesticides is determined, a process in which the primary concern must always be saftey.

Style

Clarity

A writer's style is always at some level shaped by her purposes, and these can usually be identified without too much difficulty in a work of nonfiction. Indeed, in the case of *Silent Spring*, Carson really only has one aim: to raise public awareness about the dangers of pesticides with the ultimate goal of bringing about more prudent pest-management practices. What stylistic necessities does this task impose on the writer? The first is accessibility. If her message is aimed at the public, then she must write in a manner that is suitable for the widest possible circle of readers.

The second imperative arises from her determination not merely to inform readers but to motivate them to activism. Carson must put the case in such a way that individuals feel obliged to get involved.

Finding a style that is suitable for a general audience is tricky in writing a book like *Silent Spring* where so much technical information must be presented. The writer must make the complex comprehensible but avoid doing so in a manner that oversimplifies and therefore undermines the authority of scientific information. Carson had been doing just that for over two decades, first as a science writer for the federal government, then as a bestselling interpreter of marine biology. Not surprisingly, her technique is easiest to examine in those sections of *Silent Spring* that focus on the most complicated matters—chapters like "Elixirs of Death" (on pesticide chemistry) and "Through a Narrow Window" (on cell biology).

In these two chapters readers find chemical nomenclature ("dichlor-diphenyl-trichloroethane"!), passages on neurophysiology, debate about toxicity reckoned in "parts per million," and exotic terminology drawn from cell biology. Though one might think it counterproductive to include such language in a book aimed at a general audience, Carson is careful not to go too far, and the ultimate effect is quite positive. Not only does the scientific nitty-gritty lend the argument an irresistible objectivity and authority, but the author's own ease with this complicated material builds trust in the reader. What keeps readers afloat in this tide of esoterica (knowledge or information known only to a small group) are Carson's clear explanations. Never does she touch on a technical subject without a clarifying digression, even if it requires a paragraph or two. The unfailing success of these passages lies mainly in her ability to make the abstract concrete. For example, organic chemistry is elucidated through metaphor; the component substances are described as "building blocks" that chemists assemble into more elaborate "Lego"-like compounds. The effects of pesticides on cellular metabolism are likened to the overheating of an engine.

Persuasiveness

Carson hopes to incite her readers to action, and the scientific data, no matter how well explained, lacks the requisite emotional appeal. To get readers to care about problems like the estrogenic properties of organic chemicals and the depletion of adenine triphosphate, Carson must make them not only understandable but also meaningful.

Carson's solution is to use highly charged language to keep the human implications of the pesticide problem in the foreground. For every use of the word "herbicide," for example, there is one of "weed-killer." The following fragments are culled from just the first few pages of *Silent Spring*: "Lethal," "battery of poisons," "endless stream" of new chemicals, "violent crossfire" of pesticide use, "fanatic zeal" of pest-control agencies, "tranquilizing pills" of chemical industry disinformation, "agents of death," "havoc," "indiscriminate" spraying.

Still more striking are those passages in which Carson uses such language to paint unsettling images of acute poisoning in animals and humans: birds losing balance, suffering tremors and convulsions, and then abruptly dying; a baby vomiting, experiencing a seizure and unconsciousness, and ending up a "vegetable"; a housewife wracked by fever and never-ending joint pain. Few things affect readers as powerfully as the specter of death, and Carson conjures it again and again in *Silent Spring*. Pesticides are associated with some of people's worst fears, and she does not hesitate to exploit the connection, evoking among other things the long agony of cancer and the heartbreaking spectacle of children plagued by birth defects.

In such a fashion, the writer virtually assures that readers will become anxious about the problem. Many commentators have noted that Carson very cannily draws an analogy between pesticides and radioactive fallout, a comparison that could not have failed to unnerve readers at the height of the Cold War. But there is quite enough haunting imagery in *Silent Spring* for it to have stirred up the public even without that powerful association.

The Rise of Synthetic Pesticides

So influential a role did Carson's *Silent Spring* play in the quickening of concern about pesticides that it is often assumed that she was the first to call attention to the problem. But pesticides had been in wide use since the nineteenth century, and debates about their effects on health had been going on for decades. But the nature of the chemical threat changed dramatically after World War II, and Carson was the first popular writer to explain this development to Americans.

During the early twentieth century, the most commonly used chemical pesticides were arsenic compounds. They were deadly enough to cause a few health scares, but a far cry from the poisons that wartime chemical weapons research bequeathed to the world—an entirely new and ever expanding family of man-made toxins called organochlorines, the most notorious of which was DDT. The new pesticides were more lethal than their predecessors, more numerous, and more widely used. They also stayed toxic over a long period, accumulated in the body, and concentrated in the food chain. By the late 1950s, a handful of scientists, naturalists, and attentive citizens could hear the "rumblings of an avalanche"; ecological and public health problems of unprecedented proportion were beginning to come into view. Rachel Carson was the first to bring this emerging crisis to the attention of the general public in a compelling way.

Science, Technology, and Nature

Since the very first days of the industrial revolution, technology has always been a mixed blessing. It has helped humans to create and to destroy; it has both enriched life and impoverished it. Until perhaps the present moment, which has seen such extraordinary breakthroughs in information science, genetics, and astrophysics, the mid-twentieth century was the most dizzying era of all time on the technological front. The pace of progress, the breadth of innovation, and the size of the strides were quite unprecedented. It was the age in which humanity got its first taste of ultimate power in areas such as organic chemistry where scientists created substances that never occurred in nature, and physics, which spawned the atomic bomb.

Rapid progress has always been intoxicating, and the mid-century boom was no different in this respect. In the heady early years, it seemed that the new know-how would allow civilization to solve all of its problems. But soon this optimism disintegrated in the usual way: the physical universe turned out to be more complicated than it had appeared, and once-powerful tools rapidly exhausted their usefulness. What set this particular phase of disillusionment apart from earlier ones was civilization's recognition that, for the first time in history, technology could threaten life on a global scale. The end result was not just more modest expectations about what science could achieve at that moment, but a series of major social movements (environmentalism, the anti-nuclear movement, etc.) that saw humanity's only hope for survival in a radical reconception of its relationship to the natural world. *Silent Spring* sprang from this loss of faith in science and technology and also intensified it.

Critical Overview

Critics writing about *Silent Spring* when it first appeared disagreed very little about the author's literary gifts. An anonymous reviewer for *Life* magazine called the book vivid, a work of great "grace" by a "deliberate researcher and superb writer." *Time*'s reviewer echoed much of this praise; once again, Carson was said to be a "graceful writer" who demonstrated considerable "skill in building her frightening case." In assessing the book's claims, however, the early reviews were sharply divided. Periodicals aimed at birders and other nature-oriented readers, who likely already knew something about dangers of pesticides, found Carson's argument unassailable. The mainstream press, on the other hand, was skeptical on the whole. Some of the resistance stemmed from a natural reluctance to accept what was, after all, a shocking proposition—the technological "miracle" of pesticides, long claimed to be safe by the chemical industry and trusted government officials, was a Trojan horse that threatened life on a global scale. For example, the reviewer for *Life* found much that was compelling in Carson's "amply buttressed" argument, anxiously hoped that she had "overstated her case" in predicting widespread destruction.

> The scenes she describes so vividly
> —the neighborhood where all the
> robins perished after eating DDT-

engorged earthworms, the woman who died of leukemia after repeatedly spraying spiders in her cellar, the salmon streams emptied by seeping poisons—are all true enough. But they are isolated examples.

One can only conclude that the critic was groping for reassurance here in turning away from the obvious point of Carson's catalog of pesticide disasters, which was that the incidents alluded to were harbingers of worse, more widespread trouble. That he largely shared the author's concerns is clear enough in the review's conclusion where he called for the very same remedies that *Silent Spring* urges: tougher restrictions on pesticide use and more government funding for research.

Compare & Contrast

- **1962:** Thalidomide, often prescribed for morning sickness, is suspected of causing birth defects, adding to already widespread concern about the dangers of synthetic chemicals.

  Today: The Environmental Protection Agency requires pesticide makers to submit data that will allow the agency to determine the special risks of their products for children.

- **1962:** Watson, Crick, and Wilkins

win a Nobel Prize for describing the molecular structure of DNA.

Today: Scientists complete a provisional map of the entire human genome.

- **1963:** President Lyndon Johnson signs the Clean Air Act, legislation designed to protect air quality in the United States.

Today: The United Nations agree to the Kyoto Protocol, a plan for reducing emission of greenhouse gases.

Not all of the skeptical reviews were as friendly as *Life* magazine's; *Silent Spring* was the target of a well-funded smear campaign by the chemical industry, and a startling number of the early critics align themselves with that effort in one way or another. Indeed, in a magazine as influential in the shaping of public opinion as *Time*, there appeared a review that so harmonized with the position of pesticide makers that its author, if he was not in fact an industry hatchet man, might as well have been. Calling Carson a "hysterical" woman, the reviewer employed the industry's favorite attack on her and then presented fragments of some of the harshest passages of *Silent Spring* in an attempt to make its author seem unbalanced. For example, he cited her "emotion fanning" claim that DDT is found in mother's milk and her claim that people "can't add pesticide to water anywhere without threatening the purity of water everywhere." Elsewhere the distortions are even more pronounced, as where he called the writer's advocacy of biologic pest management "reckless primitivism." So egregious are the misreadings and lapses that it is hard not to conclude that the review's object was damage control, not rational debate about the issue.

Since the publication of *Silent Spring*, critical opinion of the book has changed in three important ways. First, no one questions the soundness of Carson's argument anymore; forty years of scientific research has confirmed virtually all of the book's major claims. The second change is related to the historical importance of *Silent Spring*, often called the *Uncle Tom's Cabin* of modern environmentalism. In "The Reception of *Silent Spring*, " Craig Waddell offered one of the most concise assessments of the book's significance.

> Ernest Hemingway once wrote that " [a]ll modern American literature comes from one book by Mark Twain called *Huckleberry Finn.*" It would not be too much of an exaggeration to make a similar claim for *Silent Spring*'s relationship to the modern environmental movement. Although the American environmental movement traces its roots to such nineteenth-century visionaries as Henry David Thoreau,

George Perkins Marsh, and John Muir—all of whom were concerned with the preservation of the wilderness—the modern environmental movement, with its emphasis on pollution and the degradation of the quality of life on the planet, may fairly be said to have begun with one book by Rachel Carson called *Silent Spring*.

Today, more and more critics are turning their attention to historical considerations. Several examples of such work appear in a recently published anthology of essays called *And No Birds Sing;* for instance, Ralph Lutts argues that the book's initial popularity was in some large measure attributable to the panic over atomic fallout, and Cheryll Glotfelty shows how Carson's critique of "man's [pesticide] war against nature" exploits the tropes of Cold War discourse.

The third major change in the criticism of *Silent Spring* might be guessed from comparisons of Carson's book to *Uncle Tom's Cabin* and *Huckleberry Finn.* Having earned a place among the American classics for its historical significance, it is now the object of the close textual scrutiny always given to such works. *Silent Spring* is treated as a literary text across the usual range of interests: in "An Inventional Archaeology," Christine Oravec looks at Carson's manuscript to learn about the book's composition; Edward Corbett's "A Topical Analysis" examines the argument through the lens of classical rhetoric; and " *Silent Spring* and Science Fiction" by Carol Gartner points to its generic kinship with science fiction. Given Carson's considerable talents as a writer, this recent interest in literary dimensions of *Silent Spring* seems on the whole a promising development.

Sources

Brooks, Paul, "Rachel Louise Carson," in *Notable American Women: The Modern Period,* Harvard University Press, 1980, pp. 138-41.

Corbett, Edward P. J., "A Topical Analysis of 'The Obligation to Endure,'" in *And No Birds Sing: Rhetorical Analyses of Rachel Carson's "Silent Spring,"* Southern Illinois University Press, 2000, pp. 60-72.

"The Gentle Storm Center," in *Life,* Vol. 53, October 1962, pp. 105-106.

Glotfelty, Cheryll, "Cold War, *Silent Spring:* The Trope of War in Modern Environmentalism," in *And No Birds Sing: Rhetorical Analyses of Rachel Carson's "Silent Spring,"* Southern Illinois University Press, 2000, pp. 157-73.

Killingsworth, M. Jimmie, and Jacqueline S. Palmer, " *Silent Spring* and Science Fiction: An Essay in History and Rhetoric of Narrative," in *And No Birds Sing: Rhetorical Analyses of Rachel Carson's "Silent Spring,"* Southern Illinois University Press, 2000, pp. 174-204.

Lear, Linda J., "Rachel Louise Carson," in *American National Biography,* Oxford University Press, 1999, pp. 474-76.

Lutts, Ralph, "Chemical Fallout: *Silent Spring,* Radioactive Fallout, and the Environmental Movement," in *And No Birds Sing: Rhetorical*

Analyses of Rachel Carson's "Silent Spring," Southern Illinois University Press, 2000, pp. 17-41.

Oravec, Christine, "An Inventional Archaeology of 'A Fable for Tomorrow,'" in *And No Birds Sing: Rhetorical Analyses of Rachel Carson's "Silent Spring,"* Southern Illinois University Press, 2000, pp. 42-59.

"Pesticides: The Price for Progress," in *Time,* Vol. 80, September 1962, pp. 45-48.

Sale, Kirkpatrick, *The Green Revolution: The American Revolution, 1962-1992,* Hill and Wang, 1993, pp. 25 and 94.

Steingraber, Sandra, *Living Downstream: An Ecologist Looks at Cancer and the Environment,* Addison-Wesley, 1997, pp. 31-117.

Waddell, Craig, "The Reception of *Silent Spring:* An Introduction," in *And No Birds Sing: Rhetorical Analyses of Rachel Carson's "Silent Spring,"* Southern Illinois University Press, 2000, pp. 1-16.

Further Reading

Graham, Frank, *Since "Silent Spring,"* Houghton Mifflin, 1970.

> Graham's book offers a detailed account of the pesticide controversy that followed the publication of *Silent Spring*.

Lear, Linda, *Rachel Carson: Witness for Nature,* Henry Holt & Co., 1997.

> *Rachel Carson: Witness for Nature* is widely regarded as the definitive biography of Carson.

Waddell, Craig, ed., *And No Birds Sing: Rhetorical Analyses of Rachel Carson's "Silent Spring,"* Southern Illinois University Press, 2000.

> The essays in this volume all focus on the language of *Silent Spring*, not always from the standpoint of the rhetorician, as the title suggests, but in the manner of literary critics more generally—one examining Carson's manuscripts for clues about the her intentions, another attempting to classify the book in terms of genre, *etc.*

Wargo, John, *Our Children's Toxic Legacy: How Science and Law Fail to Protect Us from Pesticides,* Yale University Press, 1996.

As the book's title indicates, Wargo asks whether current pesticide regulations adequately safeguard children, but *Our Children's Toxic Legacy* also provides an excellent overview of the pesticide problem, including a detailed description of the contemporary regulatory process. Along with Steingraber's *Living Downstream,* Wargo's book is essential reading in this area.

CPSIA information can be obtained
at www.ICGtesting.com
Printed in the USA
LVOW13s1344190118
563208LV00010BA/14/P

9 781375 399869